FIRST COMES LOVE

First Come Love

Pino Coluccio

Mansfield Press

Library and Archives Canada Cataloguing in Publication

Coluccio, Pino
    First comes love / Pino Coluccio.

Poems.
ISBN 1-894469-21-6

    I. Title.

PS8605.O493F57 2005   C811'.6   C2005-901926-3

Design: Denis De Klerck, Marijke Friesen
Cover Photo: Hendrick Frank / iStockphoto

The publication of *First Comes Love*
has been generously supported by
The Canada Council for the Arts and
The Ontario Arts Council.

Mansfield Press Inc.
25 Mansfield Avenue, Toronto, Ontario, Canada. M6J 2A9
Publisher: Denis De Klerck
www.mansfieldpress.net

for Rachel

CONTENTS

Some guys have all the luck
Some guys have all the pain
Some guys get all the breaks
Some guys do nothing but complain

J. Fortgang

THE CEO OF HEAVEN

Our first production schedule gave us
thirteen days, not six,
to roll the earth and heavens out.
But when the moon and lakes

and mountains led to overruns
I had to change the mix
and scrap a lot of the bells and whistles—
why swaths of sun and sex

were clipped clean out of Canada
and Niger's on the rocks,
and way more women buy their bras
at Wal-mart than at Saks.

But Beelzebub,
my go-to guy, to fix
the bad P.R.—always thinking
right outside the box—

raised the bar. He tweaked our working draft of man
by palming him an apple.
"*C'est fou, la vie*," he says. "But smile—
one bite will make you able."

SALT INSTEAD OF SEED

The boy who's lit the lamp again to read
notices a shadow on the snow.
His father's, sowing salt instead of seed

along the walk, who's stopped to pick a bead
of breath that's frozen to his scarf. Although
the boy has lit the lamp to read

he wonders how it would have felt to weed
the beans his father used to grow,
the father sowing salt instead of seed

past the house, who's stumbled on a need
now to dim both the kitchen's cozy glow,
and him, the boy who's lit the lamp to read.

For though the boy had started as a sort of greed
by proxy, that led the man to leave behind his hoe,
the father sowing salt instead of seed

sees a page turn, sees the boy proceed
to chapter one. And knows he doesn't know
the boy who's lit the lamp to read.
The father's sowing salt instead of seed.

Shopping

1

Subway-rides away, a few choose
the burnished brick of Yorkville boutiques,
where supermodels sample chic shoes—
Manolos or nothing—and golf pros
and clerks claim speedy-shuttered peeks
at the shadowed curves of feet in shiny hose.

2

The wide windows dressed with crisp blouses
(melon reds, lemon yellows, creams)
are TV screens—but not the ones in houses.
Ones instead you enter, where *you* become
the star. Living rooms where TV dreams
are real: that's what malls are. For some.

3

Honest Ed's. Kerchiefed cowling mothers
thumb denims, poke thin plaids,
soon joined by stooping plumpy others,
purses on their wrists, who ponder wares
like pictures at exhibits. Heating pads
will wait. They rummage after graver cares.

Getting In

It wasn't bugs buzzing but the lights,
which few of us had seen before. The Queen
was on the wall behind the desk. Nights
of bad roads had come to this: men

in line for miles, guessing how it stands.
Reap three fields of wheat and weed the peppers –
we sweated seven shirts. And for our papers?
Hands was all they said. Show us your hands.

We caught on quick. They wanted men for work.
Our hands—we held them out—were hard as bark.
We eyed each other nervously, and then?
Hands was all they said. We all got in.

OLIVE JARS

1

They couldn't stop me always
    gobbling olives.
I'd peep and creep in socks
    on eager toes,
past watchful work boots
    all in rows,
in the house where still today
    my tiny ma lives.

2

Barstools always turned
    to me their backs
in the basement where I hopped
    the tiles' cracks
to the room I helped my pa
    and brother build,
the dark *cantina*, cramped
    and winter-chilled.

3

I tugged the lone bulb's
    silver chain.
The naked joists above me
    swayed and swept,
branches dangling down
    then up again
gory salted meats
    that always kept.

4

I rub my eyes but see them
       even now,
and sniff the squat vats
       on plinths of pine,
the burping vats fermenting
       frothy wine,
a blinking kid in wonder
       at just how.

5

The jars of *giardiniera*
       came next,
piquant peppers soaked
       in oil and vexed.
A glimpse and your tingling
       lips hurry
to make your wobbly stomach
       walls worry.

6

Further back on cracked
       battered planks
other jars sealed up
       basil musks,
jars of sauce in straight
       parading ranks
that plumped and glimmered red
       as summer dusks.

7

Below these, like glass
          placentas glinting,
or urns, twelve more
          jars stood.
These were filled with olives
          black and good
as ma's eyes, her hair
          before its flinting.

8

They turned earth flavours
          on your tongue,
which muscled up already,
          writhed and wrung
a pit so that your brain
          reared and chased
trees it couldn't see
          but now could taste.

9

A squelched pop, I twisted
          off a top.
The march of my molars unmuffled
          by olive lust,
my hands maintained a steady
          plop, plop
into jars, for glossy olives
          fast and fussed.

10

Lips kissed pits
        free of meat,
a final dunk of hands,
        pits hidden,
caps clapped, heavy
        jars slid in,
I tugged the cord and scurried
        in retreat.

11

I leave you now, *cantina*,
        to the years,
to the dust and dark that hide your
        empty jars,
that once kept capped
        years static,
years that scatter now
        in heaving havoc.

12

Not so much today
        the olive-gobbler,
the scraps I scratch and scratch
        and shove in drawers
I pack with olives saved
        for when I'm older,
the scraps I scratch, my only
        olive jars.

Up Here in the Scomps

Peace out to my dawgs up in Scarbados,
up in Cedarbrae and Warden Woods.
Big props to my homies in
Tuxedo Court and Malvern,
Wexford, Oakridge—all the Scarlem hoods.

Peace out to the hos who go to Thompson,
the cute Leacock coochies in Bulgari.
Big props to the gangstaz stuck
at Lam all day, and Porter,
with hoopties sooped up phat as a Ferrari.

Peace out to the playaz on McCowan,
Orton Park and Lawrence, Morningside.
Big props to the thugz with cribs
on Markham Road or Neilson,
who smoke a fat blunt and jack a ride.

Peace out to my nigz who get they fade on
drinkin beers on Friday at the party.
Big props to the crackaz makin
booty calls and frontin,
the ballaz buyin bitches mo Bacardi.

A Rouge River Ramble

Peopled only after it was planned,
our suburb's gingham picnic cloth of parking lots and plazas,
past its last subdivision's stand,

tatters to a single snaking lane. Nature reconvenes.
Fields run into woods where roots,
like knees through rips in jeans,

poke up through the packed down path that parts the forest floor.
I falter down it, not sure what
I'm looking at, or for.

Domed leaves sift the dim light.
Toppled trunks are shins a brontosaurus left behind.
The river burps beside me to my right.

And everything is ferny and unkempt,
with seedy weeds blown way out of proportion.
I gob a wad of fearful half-contempt.

Less the nearby suburb's fringe than distant nature's own
(and one you know
will be developed soon),

these woods were never painted by Tom Thomson—
                           there's tires, bags and cans,
now and then a disconcerting shoe or pair of panties,
shopping carts like ribs of aliens.

But still I find the chipmunks (out of Disney) kind of cute,
that shuck a nut, freeze,
then chew a shoot.

And wonder if there's fish still in the river,
on which reflected pine boughs
shine and shiver.

Every year I straggle to this sub-suburban patch,
victim to an itch again that heaven gets as well,
which only trees are tall enough to scratch.

Highland Dancers

Here to win,
they bow and then begin.
Tight hair,
fingers in the air
or poised on hips,
concentrating lips
and leaping feet
that tamp the piper's beat,
the stage a drum—
this is where they're from.
A swish of kilt,
taut socks on built
calves that spin,
sunless freckled skin
and cold
heat that's lively yet controlled.
But most of all,
straight necks, tall
backs—a bold
sense of owning something old.

THE VICTOR

Waves whack
and slurp the harbour wall,
silvered by the sun,
bob a duck
and reek of rusty hull.
A lot of what you see
on York Quay
is cinematic. One

year I worked
down here, catching
lines for vessels coming
in. And perked
up for Shelly, the fetching
first mate aboard
the Victor. Weird.
Her shoulder muscles humming,

she'd swab the deck,
super well-accoutered
for standard sex appeal,
her legs and neck
long. But what mattered
more than her tight,
sail-white
teeth was her role

as sailor: telling
the wind and waves what
to do had made her more
her own. Quailing,
I loved it when she'd pat
me on the back, park
her shoe and bark
at me to tie it, or wear

me as a balance.
And this I doubt myself:
as if it had been planned,
she noticed once
that something smudged her calf.
To scrub it, without lather,
but a bather
by Degas, she bent

and by mistake?—
she had me hold the hose.
My heart pulled a skid.
Her lingering look
measured how right she was,
whether she drove me wild.
When she smiled,
I knew she knew she did.

First Comes Love

There comes a time when sitting home alone
looking at your life—"I'm such a knob"—
gets to be a drag. You hate your job,
your car's a piece of crap, and what you eat
is fatty, fried and salty. But then you meet
a girl; the life you've made a mess of pulses.
And not content to mess up just your own,
you settle down and mess up someone else's.

HOME

The lengths people go to long for home.
Everything I hated while I had it down the street
I'm achy for in Rome.

Or would be if I went, I'm willing to bet.
Talking proper. Knowing the quickest way
from A to B. The safety net

of parents. And a past—places I have memories
of, like where I first saw Lindsey, and where we first
went out. My favourite snacks and toiletries

like Chips Ahoy! and Dove, I doubt if Roman
supermarkets carry. And theme songs like "The Flintstones"
they won't ever recognize. It's something deeply human

to see the beach as sandier on someone else's shore.
But even if our skies are grey, our girls are mostly dowdy,
and even if our football is a bore—

me, I'll drop my fruits where I was planted.
Home is not for leaving and then loving from afar,
but living in and totally taking for granted.

CHILDHOOD

Uncles and mothers
say always treat others
how you would like *them* to treat *you.*

"But masochists can't,"
I said to my aunt.
She gave me a bruise and it's blue.

Adulthood

For ten years, hornier than lonely;
then adulthood. Youth is a long convalescence,
adulthood a rueful looking back to what was only
a badly botched attempt at adolescence.

YEARBOOK

Tiger, Wayne and Jordan play the jock.
The brain is Bill Gates. The moody kid
no one's heard talk, Mohammed Atta,
frowns at Brit, who leads us into cheers.
Life fits the pattern of the years

you spent in school. For Andy Schorr and Marlon
Ketcham too, whose dark nods in crowded
halls, seeming to beg or blame, I saw
every day but didn't see. And Lynne Perdue,
whose made-up face and earrings were for me

though, irked at my deserving her affection,
I feigned not to notice. What're they up to
now? What slow door has locked them
out of all that could have been, the starring
role and final-minute win?

Once exams and essays are all through,
you never think of them, their unuplifted
faces, some caught in blinks, that fill
the yearbook. There's never any need until—
you realize they never think of you.

This Week in Verse

Monday

GO Trains and elevators lurk,
that whisk me to the top of my autonomy:
the cubicle, the terminal—the work—
that make of me a dime in the economy.

Tuesday

I left the stuffy office for some air,
but choked:
a seamy-headed temp had beat me there—
who smoked.

Wednesday

There's two kinds (and fate is unforgiving):
those who live, and those who make a living.

Thursday

It's 5:45 and the subway is solid
with elbows and raincoats. Commuting is squalid.
I'm headed for home. I'm nervous and glum.
And someone's umbrella is poking my bum.

Friday Night

Why's it got me down that she's with him
over in the corner where it's dim?
Not because it's lonely here alone.
It's just I wasted putting on cologne.

20

THE FIREWORKS DISPLAY

Escalators boost us to Bolero
on a sax. We elbow on at Bloor
and bustle south. Camping on a sewer
once we get there, pocked Natives zero
in and pan. It's hard not to feel
like a groundling at the Globe: uppers
looking down from Harbour Castle suppers
catch me looking up. Toe-to-heel,
jostled, I check the time. Bands delay,
TV people spoon it with a fork,
and Mayor Mel: a version of New York
until it starts, the fireworks display—
corked stars and comets popping free,
falling like the former century.

2002

The same kids, though out alone and later;
the love that's turned to worry more than warmth.
The same house squatting on its lot
and hunkered car that hustles him to work.
The same job. And breathing loud in sleep
beside him, the same wife. Happy two thousand
and two. A new year, the same life.

STANDARDS

The bony babes in Gap who lazily
stroll with Starbucks cups at U of T,
Photoshopped or bio-engineered,
see me dreamy-eyed and think I'm weird.

And then, with bosky dos and shoes from Browns,
the tall and toothsome daughters wearing frowns
who sit in Yorkville sipping Chardonnays
squirmily avert my swimming gaze.

But me, no matter how desperate I get,
my standards will never descend
to hairy-legged fatties or anyone else
who'd settle for me, and pretend.

THINGS TO DO

Lists of things to do: it's glum
to think of what they all become,
lists of things you never got
around to, or never gave a shot.
You panic. Will I fit it in?
The little time you have to do it
ticks. Ready to begin,

you find a reason not to. Screw it.
Most of it you never mean
to do. Kitchenettes to clean,
the laundry, movies to return:
fine. But lose weight, learn
French, or take up violin;
move to Montreal: you grin

and shiver. These are not a list
of open nets you somehow missed,
but only hide the wall of what
you are, like art graffitied on
of something nicer. Mow the lawn
is good. Or hair: get it cut.
But study law at Queen's or ask

Lindsey Love out mask
how little life is yours to will.
Watch. Soon the past will fill
the future in. Life will shut
you out. Your plans will be a blur.
What will you become? What
else: what you always were.

All Is Vanity

I try but can't get near her;
something comes between—
I mean her mirror.
I curse her and complain
but only ugliness
would call her vain.
Which isn't it at all.
Looking down on isn't—
if you're tall—

condescending,
and acting like you're better
is not pretending
if you are.
We aren't all the same
make of car.
The Chevy Cavaliers
and other heaps that fill
the lot at Sears

or KFC are dreamers
if they dream of
being Bimmers.
I think of her at night.
No one likes her half
as much as me
except herself,
who nature gave the right
to vanity.

GOOD

At six or seven even then
already she was good. I'd show up
wearing yesterday's spaghetti
on my shirt to ask her could
she play with me. She could. But first she had

to water. For Saturday was hot
and Sunday hotter, and all her mother's
marigolds were limp, her mother's
purple columbines were stoopy,
the hollyhocks beside her house

could barely lift their leaves, her mother's
purple irises were droopy.
I'd hide inside the shade on her
veranda, coveting the bumble
bee or panda on her shirt,

ironed on and giving glitzy
twinkles. I'd sit and cross my ankles
on the rings of dirt around them,
and stow the lonely underlife
of neediness for love that's much

a part of growing up, as much
as cake or Christmas. We'd shove, soon,
her little bike with streamers in
its grips off its wonky stand
and double far. But first she tipped

the hydro pole a drink, the hydro
pole that hadn't sprouted branches
from its trunk. "Maybe it'll
grow someday. It could." And this
was most of all what made her good.

LINDSEY

Wooed by bigger, cooler guys,
she wasn't about to offer me
her cuppably-curvy cheekbone-peaks,
but set about it generously,
waving hi, her sweater plush,
when she'd pass me in the hall

and sitting beside me in class. Of all
the beautiful girls I've met,
the only one I can't forget
is Lindsey. Lindsey's denim thighs,
her glasses (jutting past her cheeks),
hairclip (blue to match her eyes)

and tapered waist's petiteness;
her cola bob, soon blush
and voice's April sweetness—
that weren't beauty's bright disguise
for shoulds she'd disregarded.
Lindsey mild and lovely-hearted.

CLUBFOOT

Miss, watch these youngsters chase
that yellow butterfly.
The one who dusts his fingers first
then lets it go will never thirst or sigh

at night for limbs and lips and love:
they'll settle on his forearm while he sleeps.
The one who, having caught
it late, keeps

it under pins, will end up either
early dead, insane, in debt or drunk. I
was one when young
who never caught the butterfly,

as once your love, Miss,
did a little dip and pirouette,
then do-si-doed a skimmy
from my net.

But butterflies and youngsters, love
and Miss, your silhouette,
once this sun it shows
against has set,

will disappear. Lighter butterflies
will flutter by, where none can watch,
that even on this clubfoot
I will (cup my hands and) catch.

HUNCHBACK

Talking long and spoons of soup fog
the kitchen window. And so their lives combine.
Their love is less a dot and more a line.
He pulls her light warm weight upon
his chest and soft sighs commingle—
good old same old same old. Medium bliss
and fought-for sweetest tedium, parting kiss
and call and welcome touch,
durable daily nothing much
and endless happy tingle—
these are theirs alone to own
and offer.
        A hunchback, seven city blocks away,
loops a lanky arm around his dog.
The news is on. Pastrami's drooling mustard on his tray.

The Wedding Charter

Beside the former terminal warehouse,
now a tony mall I threaded towards the cold of
to beat the soggy thickness of July,
another boat was boarding for a charter,
frumped up in center pieces,
coloured table cloths,
and sadly homey helium balloons.
I chuffed at first but when I read
the flexing banner pulled across the bow—
"Congrats Ben & Lindsey"—
I stopped to join the other shaded faces looking on.
The restless water's soft insistent pat smelling rusty,
the wide horizon's flat,
the tall sky and unobstructed breeze
unlocking for an afternoon the traffic's static heat
plucked the groom from ducking under limits.
Squat legs sinister with sex
scissored out of slits in glitzy dresses,
rippled arches bulging out of slinky satin sandals
clomped to upper decks,
and mothers waved, grinning at successes:
a mix of us in running shoes and shorts waved back.
And then the bride was whisked aboard,
her swan's-feather bodice flaring white,
and my lip and chintip quivered.
A whistle startled seagulls into flight,
summer hands unhitched the heavy gang and dropped the lines,
dock attendants slipped them from their bollards,
and slow as dreamy drifting—
"To matrimony's latest inductees!"—
the faux steamer chugged the couple off.
I stood there in their wake.
They squinnied at the unconverging blueness of the lake
that met them as they exited the harbour.
And just before the bushy islands blocked them from my view,
two taut and yellow specks nuzzled pertly upwards,
balloons unnoosed and borne above the clouds.

Where Has All the Mayo Gone?

Hungry late I clank around
the kitchen for a snack.
A pickle first and then why not
I peel apart a pack

of luncheon meat, some Swiss, a leaf
of something limp and wan.
And now oh no the lid's on tight
but look—the mayo's gone.

It feels like only yesterday
I parked my father's car
and peeked at other shoppers' carts
and tootled to a jar

for slathering on hot dogs
and for dolloping on frites—
there's loads of foods whose fatty goodness
mayonnaise completes.

My pumpernickel won't go down.
It's like a warning bell,
the chilly clink of stainless steel
on glass. I know it well.

And wonder under nibbles
if at bottom human lives
aren't always scraping empty jars
with tips of pointless knives.

The Mouse

He kept well walled the crumbs he'd take,
whether of bread or birthday cake.
And Cheerios were bagels to
the mouse who watched our doings through
a vent, but scruffled late at night
in the glowy dim of the blue half-light
that LEDs in VCRs
(which appear, to mice, as stars
appear to humans) softly shed
on mice out for their nightly bread.
Like all who hide, he walled less well
the funky crisp small carcass smell
that carried, when the furnace coughed,
through the lonely downtown loft
where silence asked me and its friend
the dark why lives lived little, end.

Aging Men

In time they sink to wrinkledness and slumping,
men who years ago were taut and broad.
As choads have a heft to them in humping
that shrivels when they slobber up their wad.

Chipper glans, your goopy dribble gleams.
You lose your load as aging men their dreams.

Drinking Song

Shoulder-to-shoulder,
they stand at attention,
bottles behind a bar.

Generals stooped on stools
give orders;
bottles march to war.

Pain gets hurt,
and truth and sensitivity
and thought

desert, and gin
and whiskey win
the battle, shot by shot.

It happens every
Friday. Payday
generals out on benders

raise a glass
to victory;
tomorrow, sign surrenders.

Something in the Attic

Envy of my betters up
on higher floors than me
often gets me down.
The sweeping city vistas
they can swivel back and see,
their meetings with renown,

the P.A.'s brewing light and lively
blends who screen their calls,
freckled leggy models.
And beaming family faces
by the frameful on their walls.
I dab their dewy wattles,

a ninetofiving numbercruncher
skirting why or how
(habit, yes, and fear).
The cubicle I started in
I still report to now—
a heifer's stalled career.

But necessary lies arrive,
dependably indelible:
I'm something in the attic.
Dusty in the quiet dark,
unusefully unsellable.
But comfortably static.

THE MRS.

The bar scene is a poor man's TSE.
I edge in, dressed (I tell myself) the part.
Babes broker tail instead of assets.
Coin glints its more than two flat facets.
The shares I sink my heart in when, a flirt,
I court disaster, never show returns.
Risk-averse, I quaff. My ulcer burns.
Some increase their holdings here. Not me.

I dawdle home to Harriet not waiting,
my dank-wattled forty-seven-tonner.
The nun I made, a life ago, my bride
to end the messy lucklessness of dating
is snoring, arms spread out, not crucified
so much as, yes, a cross. I'm saved upon her.

Our Town

When tourists call it clean
I thank them and dismiss it.
Our city's pretty livable
but why do people visit?

Streetcars ply our upright
miles of mirrored banks,
where cleaning ladies glide
at night like fish in tanks,

or grate past painted windows
where piglets hang on hooks
that clench their tiny teeth,
their soft uneyeballed looks

accusing till you scootle
where charter vessels chug
with passengers in turtlenecks
and blazers looking smug.

But winter in our city,
the only weather worse
is summer's clingy thickness
that only Freon cures.

Our ivied isle of quiet,
tony U of T,
is nice but when you're late
so's the TTC.

None of what Canada's known for,
cedar, spruce and moose,
Muskoka chairs, the Bluenose,
makes people sign our lease.

Money's what they're here for,
a merciless amount.
Dollars can be counted.
What can't be doesn't count.

Our many multiplexes
are lit up from L.A.
and KFC, the Gap—
our moods are made away.

The people here who like it
aren't from Amsterdam,
or Prague or Honolulu,
but Orangeville. To them

there's grit and grandeur here,
they like the hum and glitz.
But they go home for Christmas.
Their mothers knit them mitts.

For households in our city
home is somewhere else—
Pakistan or Portugal.
Their village pride is false

(since after all they left)
but makes them damn Toronto—
"I live here cuz I have to,
not because I want to."

No one really lives here.
It's only where we work.
I don't like it either
but can't afford New York.

THE FINGER

Long after looks have left
horniness will linger.
Growing old is nature's way
of giving us the finger.

And though our wealth and wisdom
might be sticking out our tongue,
the only way to give the finger back
is dying young.

Sounds Like Summer

I live on a dead-end street.
After ten o'clock
nobody who's still awake
takes a walk.

The stars above my porch
aren't the sparks on charred cloth
you get on camping trips.
Streetlights draw the moth.

But still it's dark enough that soon
I listen more than look.
Crickets in the bristly
grasses tick.

Air conditioners hum in yards
and cars coasting by
sound like surf.
A jumbo scrapes the sky.

You never really notice what
you are until, like a star
a galaxy away,
it's only what you were

and now it's gone. Each day
makes a bigger gap
between the man's world
and boy's map.

But will be will be were.
Regrets are emotional slumming.
What you are you've always
been becoming.

Lager leaving a bottle glugs,
fizzes as I fill
my glass. Killing time
it's me myself I kill.

Caught between the day ahead,
the one behind,
couples snuff the news and slope
to bed, though disinclined.

Bon Voyage

A kind of tugged mummy
gauze, except they're faded
asphalt, running runways
spin us free.
Clouds yield to sunrays

and dead lives drop.
It's work and bills in abeyance
we go to when we travel,
we go to see
accustomed modes unravel.

Weathered cabbies wonder
that we wonder at
the travertine in Rome,
as bland to them
as brick to us at home.

But quick convictions start
about the life I might have had—
the shoes and *motorini*,
the Venus in
that fountain from Fellini.

I check into a mustard-yellow
suite and former selves
unbutton with my shirt—I'm new.
Which may be why
I'm far from homesick—screw

the life that's waiting like
my plants for my return—
and dread getting back.
There won't be room,
no matter how I pack,

in tight routines
for classical perspectives.
And pencils come to mind,
that leave themselves
in what they leave behind.

L'AMERICANO

after Giovanni Pascoli

A woozy molten June.

A *motorino* sputters
up the street, flies
scatter, bored sheep
blink, bright shutters
clap to keep
the heat out, snoozing eyes
desert the afternoon.

The *maresciallo* mails
a yellow letter. "All
the seafood in your diet,"
a megaphone exhales,
"come and buy it,
come and buy it!" Quick small
brushes dot maroon

across the sky, high

above the tamarisk,
a rose, some pomegranate,
a distant thresher's hum,
the flour mill's brisk
electric thrum,
the whittled old men who man it
standing idly by.

Where had I landed? The bells
told me where, the yacking
kitchen's dark,
the tart sauce smells
and dog's bark
at some *americano* picking
past with lowered eye.

NONNO

Dramatic with remarks about his death—
"The old country has my heart but this one,
this one gets my bones and last breath":
that's nonno. I'm his only grandson

but keep scarce. Confession: it's the smell.
The phone brings the cackles of my aunts:
"How's the nonno?"—"Ah, he's well, he's well!"
I lie. "He doesn't eat, he shits his pants,"

would make them nervous. I know, it's a sin
the way I talk. But listen, nonno himself
wishes he could die. Seven years he's been
tucked in bed like something on a shelf

you can't use, can't sell, but can't
discard either. "*Non ce la fazzo cchiu'*,"
he whimpers, when ma and my sister Rose and aunt
Lia stand him up and sponge the blue

slug between his legs. "*Penitenza*,"
they all agree. He's doing penance for having
always sworn at and slapped Nonna Enza.
And ma and Rose and Zia Lia, shaving,

washing sheets, spooning gruel three
times a day: the best thing for them
too. Ma could take a trip, see
things, live finally. He gathers phlegm,

spits on the ceramic. I sit and watch.
A bag of dried figs rests angled
on his chest. Above the covered couch,
olive trees slant grey and crinkled;

white huts and rubble on a hill:
a blown-up colour print of Buonalbergo. Sheets
fall rumpled on his gut, rise and fall.
Veins skirt his knuckles like the streets

you strain up but skid and shuffle down
back there. I am nonno's rib.
I come from him. All his face a frown,
nonno dribbles mush down his bib.

"*Mene bascio!*" ma snarks, and later,
"When will it end?" Atlas, shouldering the past.
Trans-Atlantic aunts' cellular chatter:
"*Non te mortifica*'," it can't last."

ANOTHER LIFE AND DEATH

His joys were sparse and small,
like grass on a rocky hill.

He was young when he'd made the last
of his limited choices, and kissed

his teacher on the cheek,
and skipped an age in a week.

The wages of sin is work
in an overcoat as a poor clerk

who barters his peak and prime
for time-and-a-half overtime.

Wine, with its logic that logic
knows nothing of, silly and tragic,

crunches out QED lists
of wives with black eyes and red wrists.

His certainties started to dim
when the hurt, in turn, turned and hurt him.

He retired (he'd paid off the house)
and crouched between craving and price.

"He'd been a bright light in his youth,
burning for beauty and truth,"

but debts and dependents had quelled him.
Age brought him insights, but seldom.

Two of his girls had disowned him.
Only his youngest still phoned him.

His life, like most mostly rotten,
when it ended, was quickly forgotten.

Snails

Here come snails to crowd the walk,
each with its shiny china cargo,
its conch locket shell. No embargo
hopping hungry robins guard will block

their incremental plod across the dawn;
no bill will split the sealed secret
their soggy bodies stopper. Sails set,
they ply the pale cement from lawn to lawn.

ETHICS

1

When Hungry, going postal, eats a
seventh greasy slice of pizza,
Full parks on Hungry's gut and quarrels—
"Greedy glutton." That's the way it is.
When seltzer tablets plop and fizz,
Hungry's bad, Full's the one with morals.

2

"Listen Heart, is and ought to be
aren't really far apart,"
says the head. "And far apart
and close together, and head and heart
as well: they're all a false dichotomy."

Thinking twice, "Head," replies the heart,
"maybe they are a false dichotomy.
Or maybe they ought to be."

Making Capicollo

I. *Preliminary*

The sink was filled all week
with vermiform pig bowels.
Ma would toss orange peels
in to keep down the reek.

The dark *cantina* was a tight morgue
for cold fat loaves of pork
rolled in bulk salt and rough.
A glimpse, and I went all stiff.

The day came and ma was tooled
well: scissors, towels, cord
ranged in reach. She gave the word.
I moved off to do as told.

II. *Wine Bath*

First you had to give the things a bath
in a full pail of pa's purple wine.
The surface salt splashed off quick. Smooth
strands of pig began to shine.

But not the soaked-in stuff. You'd have wrung
and briskly slapped and poked like some masseuse
an hour, and your busy hands would have hotly stung,
to ever shake the soaked-in deep salt loose.

The cowards wavered. You kept your grip slack
or the slick things slipped away, you found,
when you plunked them down on long platters, *plack*,
and eyed them, blunt bloody mounds of wound.

III. *Bowels*

Nothing is grosser than bowels.
You lift them out in fists
with ma from the sink
and set them out on towels.
They slither down your wrists
oozing mucous, and stink
and feel like worms and snails,
dense slobber in strands
the snipping scissors squish
through. Tacky trails
remain on straining hands.
Slippy and flippy as fish,
they glisten, slick socks,
the ends of them like lips,
once you've cut them up;
and each one gawks
when flexing fingertips
stretch them wide as a cup
around a stump of meat.
Then it's pack and poke
and squeeze, shove and tuck:
you make intestines eat
like snakes that never choke
but bloating wide, suck
and gulp whole eggs
in a long, slow swallow.
Done. Tie them with cord
and you get ma's legs,
chunky, varicose and yellow.
The *cantina* will turn them hard.

The Time We Won the Cup in '82

Little guys who lug a crooked square
and campanile, and forklift debts,
deal hands and fold out butts,
Bics and joshes at haunts on St. Clair.
They down regrets and coffee swigs and clap
a buddy's back, or grin their big mouth
around a *sangwidge*, here, there, both
at once and nowhere, or nowhere you can map.
But fists and flags and long honks from rusty
Buick boats. Pop tunnels drains.
And TTC's it home at night beat.
But that day we filled the skinny street,
and next day the dailies, like all the dusty
jugs of blood that filled our skinny veins.

THE ROMA SENIORS' CLUB

for Sam Lo Tufo

A few folding chairs and lots of heads:
that was the Roma Seniors' first meeting.
Then came tables, smooth and white as beds,
bocce out back, a kitchen and better heating.

Rack lighting, a bar and a new P.A.
were added next; now folk groups play.
Heads repeat old stories like prayers.
A few heads and lots of folding chairs.

DIMENSIONS

TV's made you plump.
White hair
and polyester frump

say to write you off.
And so I shut the door
against your cough.

What I wouldn't give
to travel to
the way you used to live,

to see you in a dress
and kerchief, a barefoot
little shepherdess

or leaning on a hoe,
ballsier but like
a Bouguereau.

You cough and shatter that.
And cough again,
refusing to be flat,

insisting on dimensions
that your past, no matter
that extensions

of it reach to even
now—the clumsy way
you hold a pen—

can't contain. I bring
a glass of water to a living,
dying thing.

THE PORTRAIT

With a look that looks concerned or bitter
glimmering out of its glossy eyes,
the portrait sort of seems to regret
a loss. See how it searches and tries
to remember and urges us not to forget

the woman who was the portrait's sitter?

BELLS

after Giovanni Pascoli

What've they got, the bells?
They ping and tinkle close
but further off, their tolls

are low. A hymn that goes
gold and silver in turn
distresses the edge of a snooze.

With arcs that sort of mourn,
they implore, the bells of gold,
a sky that starts to burn.

Their canticles are cold,
their tapped tinny squeals
seem to suffer, "Yield,"

they seem to say, the bells
that sing in silver. A sound
stuck in the sky falls.

But deeper bells respond,
bells that hide. And love
that stores its strength will sound

louder from the grave.

THE CHASE

A skippy kid in buckle-ups
and woolens chasing squirrels
and grasping sunny air.
Later, thickly pompadoured,
he shows his arm to girls.

Years of chasing golden gain
of ease, the secret sum
types he'd glimpsed on upper
decks had hoarded. Types the man
had come here to become.

Now he only watches squirrels
hop and shadows spread,
his wicker at the window;
chased by unforgotten hurt
at night, and wakeful dread.

MY IMAGINARY WIFE

This is my imaginary wife.
It's lonely without someone in your life
to talk to after work about your day
and share your weekends with, or special dinners.
But real wives marry only winners
who net more than double my gross pay.

And so I made one up. I bring her flowers,
our Scrabble matches last for hours and hours—
thank God I found somebody I could marry,
gorgeous, if, it's true, imaginary.
The highway of our love is paved in years.
And when I want her to, she disappears.

Cover Band

"We can't touch Zeppelin
with our own stuff, or the Who,"
the cover band's vocalist admitted.
"It's over guys, I'm through—

mooching off of girlfriends,
semi-unemployed,
playing up in Coboconk for bikers."
(Pink Floyd.)

Nailing down the hard parts
of other people's hits
is all the fame their tiny
talent fits.

LIFE'S WORK

Breasts coned towards him (his mother's) overhead—
but he was bottle-fed.

He ogled overpasses, an apple-bright bough,
an awning. It's over now.

The soft, unsunned circles sucked by others—
tits—as if his mother's,

remain the high and hidden, the airy out of reach,
not to be his niche.

But randy crawler, cowed kid carpet-burned
and unreversed, he learned

by his liquefying dick to love as holy,
as lovely, the close and lowly,

the hard and handy everyday, the pervy but cute:
his mother's muscled foot.

And now, for 2% commission—but who'd refuse?—
he sells women's shoes.

Soap

A tighter grip on slick contours
scented to entice
will make it slip away.
Keep it cupped loose—

the slim chip you'll glide it to
will shatter when it drops.
A final frail sud,
it softly pops.

THE HARDER TALENT

His forearm guards his bottle
in plainer sorts of bar,
one man in a huddle
with what's behind his stare.

He lacks the knack for lying
that makes up such a part
of poetry and trying
to say what's in your heart,

this latter day apostle,
for whom undying truth
is told by blood and muscle
and not by tongue and tooth.

To shut your trap seems lowly
and yet the harder talent
is most times speaking truly
by staying most times silent.

CHURCH-GOER

On Sunday when I see you,
cara Rachel *bella,*
I wish, *amore mio,*
I knew the way to tell a

girl like you it pleases
me to see your face
more than it did Jesus
to bleed upon his cross.

Polaroids

Have a seat. The sweet smoky taste
of red peppers roasted over coals your aunt
Pina's fixing you will help. A crust
of bread, a glass and you'll feel better. It can't

of course bring your mother back, the good
heart she scooped from to cook for you the food
you never thought to thank her for but ate.
But taste it, Gino. See? The brightest light

she saw at night – the moon. The loudest sound
she heard before America – the thunder.
It happened to her too. Same old days
that never change, changing into years,
make you think the future is a lie.
But blow on Polaroids and it appears.

Time Piece

"Tick," it said (again), the clock.
When he listened to it talk,
seconds had the sound of feet
tapping down a darkened street.
What he scribbled, when it scanned,
seemed to have a secondhand,
and like the seconds, seemed to pace
the empty circle of time's face.
When he made it rhyme, his song,
like a cuckoo's muffled gong,
saw another hour slip
the trembling present's nervous grip.
He watched a couple in capris
trim their blue boat's sail and breeze
across the sunned-on choppy lake.
He watched a barber's scissors take
a little off the top, and hair
collect around his plump red chair.
Awake, he dreamt of them, the barber,
the blue sloop huffing towards the harbour.
And tried to keep, in what he wrote—
each word composed, each word remote,
each word a tooth in turning gears—
the time reliably for years.

Gino

A car pulls up: he sprints
across the lawn to join the boys,
Vito, Nick and Vince.
A slamming noise

and quick skid to smokes,
cologne and hair, buttoned heat,
pounded rum-and-cokes
and bleeding meat.

His father won't delay
their lucky hunt. His only warning:
the beauty of the day
is in the morning.

ACKNOWLEDGMENTS

For their contributions to this book I am grateful to the following:
Allan Hepburn, my best teacher, who got me off to a good start, and
Mariusz Walentynowicz, my best friend. I am grateful as well to
Grainc Wightman, Brendan Leach, Quido Tessel, Nick Colangelo,
Fortunato Monaco, the late Mauro Mirabella, Jiro Shirota, Andrew
Ferrari, Wayne Martins, Mike Michael, Geoff Cook, Bryan Lamb,
Carmine Starnino, Nino Ricci, Ewan White, Francesco Corsaro,
Michelangelo Sabatino, David Wright, Mimmo Baronello, Ken
MacKinnon, Madeleine Calaghan, Bill Walton, Kathleen Wilker, Gino
Di Felice, Frank Sgro, Frank Cancian, Peter Geraci, James Fernandes,
Claudette Edgehill, Sandra Medina, Zerina Crichton, Silvia Ford,
Christina Gotera, Vito Pacione, Bill Balmbra, Mike McMorrow, Jack
David, Nathan Whitlock, my brothers Albert, Mauro and Lou, all my
uncles, aunts and cousins, numerous customers over the years, and
Egidio Piccolotto and family. These friends, acquaintances, co-workers,
peers and family members have affected me in various ways, and the
book would have come out differently without them. I'd like to thank
as well, Lindsey Love, whose friendship early on inspired much of
this collection.

Earlier versions of some of these poems have appeared in *Descant,
The Danforth Review, Books in Canada* and *Maisonneuve*; I am thankful
to the editors. I thank as well my publisher Denis De Klerck.

Special thanks are due to my parents, Marzio and Maria Coluccio, for
sacrificing so much for my benefit.

Most importantly, I wish to thank Rachel Piccolotto. The unexamined
life is not worth living. Equally however, the unlived life is not worth
examining. With Rachel I really live.

Pino Coluccio lives and writes in Toronto